EXIT US!

A POETIC LOOK AT THE CHRONICLES OF QUITTING

ANTHONY J. BUTLER

EXIT US!

Anthony J. Butler's "EXIT US" creatively captures why people quit. Have you quit before? Are you thinking about quitting right now? Regardless if your reasons for leaving are a lack of support, low pay, poor leadership, problems at home, conflicts on the job and more, this book will poetically and masterfully convey the chronicles of quitting. Each poetic piece paints powerful piercing pictures that will resonate with readers professionally and personally

It's very difficult to recruit, retain and joyfully remain in work environments that keep doing the same troublesome things that push people out the door!

This must read for you and your entire staff will set the stage to engage in authentic conversations and actions across all generations. After you examine the reasons why people quit, it's up to you what you'll do with this.

Anthony shares with and learns from a variety of professionals from multiple work sectors. For speaking engagements, staff development and more, reach Anthony J. Butler at www.violenceiprevent.com

EXIT US!

EXIT US!

A POETIC LOOK AT THE CHRONICLES OF QUITTING

ANTHONY J. BUTLER

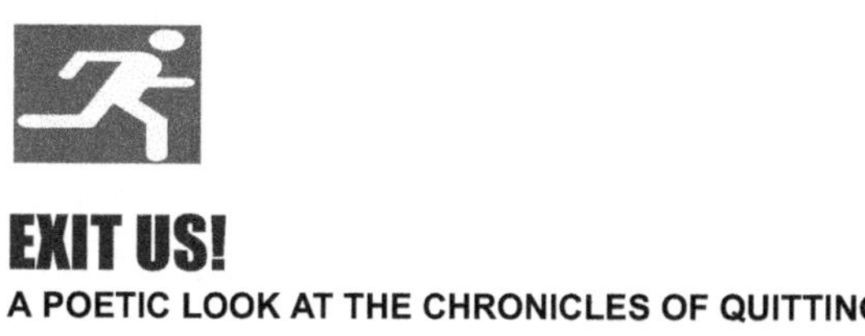

EXIT US!

A POETIC LOOK AT THE CHRONICLES OF QUITTING

Copyright © 2023 by Anthony J. Butler

To those who

Missed days
Skipped days
Used sick days
Have quit in multiple ways
Walked out or ran away
Resigned or retired sooner than
expected

EXIT US! CONTENTS

EXIT US! CONTENTS

EXIT US! CONTENTS

EXIT US! CONTENTS

THE "FOUR" WORD FOREWORD
WHY DO PEOPLE QUIT?

1. THE PANDEMIC PUSHED US
2. BIG PROBLEMS AT WORK
3. LOW PAY, HIGH DEMANDS
4. BOSSES A BIG FACTOR
5. LACK OF REAL SUPPORT
6. DISRESPECTED ALL THE TIME
7. DECIDED TO HIRE MYSELF
8. PRAYED AND HAD PEACE
9. WE COULDN'T GROW HERE
10. WAS STRESSED AND TIRED
11. WE HAVE OTHER OPTIONS
12. QUIT BEFORE BEING FIRED

When YOU Quit

When
      YOU
            Quit

When
      YOU
            finally
                  decide
                        to
                              step

This says more about YOU than the job or
career you left

Where YOU are in life plays a significant
role in knowing
when it's time for YOU to go

Not Guilty

You arrive right when you're supposed to
You time it up to leave exactly when it's
time to go… like most do
Not arriving early
Not staying late
Not doing anything extra
No longer a go getter
You might leave before the end of the hour,
day, week, month or end of the year
This job… This career
Will GUILT YOU into giving up so much
When it comes to this job or career doing a
little extra for you and giving you more…
HUSH

You pledged allegiance to your workplace,
but the workplace often doesn't reciprocate
All your years of dedication and hard work
can end instantly as you get shown the door
Not arriving early
Not staying late
Not doing anything extra
You're no longer a go getter
You are no longer bound by guilt
You are not guilty anymore
AcQUITed
NOT
GUILTY

Living Wage

Juggling bill$
Supplementing meal$
Taxed to the max
Working hard day after day…
After day… After day…
Often working off the clock unpaid
Not making a living wage
Working overtime
Sacrificing on the front line
Your pay doesn't adjust to keep up with
inflation
Living one paycheck at a time
The frustration leads you to…

Walk away with the swiftness

Quit in the middle of your shift and say
"forget this"

You post viral videos and moving messages
explaining why you had to go

Guess who decided to walk away to find a
job that paid at least a living wage?

You did

Quit Essential Reasons

Healthcare Quit: Been working double
shifts…I'm sick and tired…I'm flu with you

Church Quit: It hurts being blamed because
others don't get or make a breakthrough…
I'm pew with you

Police Quit: The defund, The disdain, The
dislike, The lose-lose… I'm blue with you

Restaurant Quit: Low pay, high stress, drive
thru and online mess… I'm food with you

Education Quit: The disrespect, discount
paychecks, tests, politics…
I'm school with you

All Work Sectors Quit: Tech-Mate…You're
outdated and antiquated…

I'm new and improved with you

One for Two and One for Three Combos

Who's appreciated for your excellence by being rewarded with more work to do?

A one for two or one for three combo with more added duties is on your menu

Far too many of your coworkers are absent and/or sub par

The sad solution… GIVE YOU THEIR WORK because you are a "STAR"

You don't mind doing more when your team is in a pinch for a few days…

However, when those few days turn into weeks, months and years…

Now look here!

You hear all the time, "Great Job" "You Are A Lifesaver" "Wonderful" and more

That's what you're told

Being great gets you multiple jobs others
refuse to hire for added to your workload

And

Your pay doesn't increase

That's cold

And

This is getting very old

You didn't ask for the one for two and one
for three combos

Who ordered this mess?

And

You're paying for the one for two and one
for three combos while others claim success

I Say… Pay… You… More

For during the jobs of 1, 2 3 and
sometimes 4

This One Person

The votes are in
The data declares
The research reveals
The common sense confirms

Leaders set the tone for who stays or leaves
This one person alone helps with Recruiting, Retention and Remaining Joyfully

Trust and believe
Leaders set the greatest tone for who stays or leaves

Titles

Tossing around titles and credentials are tell
tell signs often associated with insecurity
Many worship the titles like idols leading to
hiring others who apparently just ain't ready
Nothing against letters before and after your
name
Much respect to what you earned
However…
Actions speak louder than letters you see
AND
This is how you keep your credibility
I hope you will learn
Treat everyone with respect and value what
they suggest regardless of their title or role
Great coworkers and colleagues have a way
of dignifying all
Regardless of who can do what for them and
the titles, degrees credentials, letters and
certifications they hold

In House Fighting

In house drama
Theatrics
Theater 101
Actors and actresses playing roles
Constant conflicts and fighting
Putting out fires
Not a lot of putting in the work
High stress
Low productivity
This messy culture and climate is causing
people to bolt
Scratching, crawling, and squaring up on
site
In house fighting all day and all night

Bait and Switch

Based on the job description,
You signed up for this position
You applied for one thing and got another
Promises were made
Plush red carpet was laid in the courting and
interview stage
When you joined the team,
The bait and switch gets activated out of the
blue
Those who courted and interviewed you are
vindictive, jealous and mean now
That used to be nice person is now treating
you horribly and acting brand new
What is this?
It's the bait and switch
That's what's going down
The bait and switch

Break Out

Your first real job
You are excited
You felt great
You dreamt of working your wonders here a
long time
What?!
Wait…
You decided to walk out the door during
Thanksgiving Break
While breaking bread and eating a turkey
leg,
You decided to stretch your legs, walk away
and leave for good
What happened?!
The weight was too heavy
The daily dread was relentless
The support was consistently lacking
The red flags were waving in multiple areas
for quite awhile
You decided to break out while on break

EXIT US!
A Poetic Look At The Chronicles Of Quitting
© By Anthony J. Butler

The break,
Full of laughter and good times with family
and friends opened your eyes instantly

The break,
You decided that you won't be going back to
that dreadful, miserable job again

The break clarified things for you and now
it's time to strut in your walking shoes

The Best and Worst Leaders

Leaders…
Are you willing to put that ego on a keto
plan?

The best leaders create and cultivate an
environment of excellence
The worst leaders make the workplace a
domain of decadence
The best leaders sincerely appreciate,
congratulate, share the stage and elevate the
team
The worst leaders are haters, nasty, negative,
take all the credit, divisive and mean

The best leaders build
The worst leaders destroy

The best leaders make a move and move
many to follow them from place to place

The worst leaders have many high fiving,
hugging and shrugging when they vacate

The best leaders say what they have to say,
model, move out the way and trust you

The worst leaders micromanage, bully,
shame, blame, are hypocrites and paranoid

The worst leaders refuse to take ownership,
accept accountability and be criticized
When confronted they dodge, deflect,
enable, excuse, disrespect and give the side
eye
Not only that,
They place a target on the back of those who
oppose them, no cap, no lie

The best leaders actively listen, evaluate the
criticism, make the necessary changes,
Thank you for bringing unpleasant things to
their attention and sincerely apologize

Open Door Policy

Some leaders DEMAND respect and loyalty
you see
Some are making demands simultaneously
while they are secretly plotting to leave

When the team quits giving their all, stop
trying and don't fully buy in
Maybe they are calling in sick of the games
played, mind games and all the lying

It is a fallacy to have an open door policy
boasted up and posted up…This is strange
But…When someone takes you up on that
policy and steps to your door frame,
You keep closing and slamming doors in the
face of your team
And when they confront you on this, the
gaslighting and fake tears manifest

The staff infection is self inflicted
There is no other way to put this
This is why so many people run out the
doors, shouting…"This Is My Exit Us!"

Look and Listen

Look at their body language, posture, facial expressions and the way they walk

Listen to what they say and how they convey their frustrations when they talk

Look…Do you see them engaged and inspired?

Listen…Do you hear real recognition that is really desired?

Look…Is this a transparent workplace?

Listen…Success stories and innovative ideas… Is there plenty of sharing these?

Look…Do you see warm bodies occupying cold environments?

Listen… Ask them to describe their job or career in three words

Tally Marks

Many are counting tally marks to the end of
the week, month, or their next break

Some are walking out the door right in the
middle of the day

Not returning from the weekend festivities

They had enough of the hall of fame foolery

The revolving door of workers keeps turning
and their stay is usually short

They are screaming for help and often get
interrogated for asking for support

That's why many are counting tally marks to
the end of the week, month,
or their next break

Now Hiring

You developed a dream company laced with
your personal values and mission
You created your own job description
You skillset was perfect
You finally came to the revelation that you
can do this
You are worth it

All the blood, sweat, tears, resources, long
hours, creative thinking, complex problem
solving, critical thinking and more you did
for somebody else,

You put that same energy into YOU and
decided to promote and work for yourself
You said, "It's about time I hired myself"
You are an entrepreneur to the core
Now Hiring…
Yourself

Uncomfortable

Threats constantly being breathed down
necks
Enduring foolishness just to collect this
paycheck
Some people attempt to crush your
confidence so you can stay put
Making you think no one else will hire you,
You get comfortable
Afraid to leave
You accept this even though you know it's
not the best
You settle to be a doormat, a stool, a foot
rest
Staying stuck in a back breaking position
under someone's foot day after day
Until…
The discomfort gets unbearable and you
heroically rise up and walk away

A Typical Day

Daily disrespect
Paperwork palaces
Mountains of meetings
Never ending emails all day, all night
A flurry of furious, serious, curious, and
humorous calls
A bevy of verbal beatings
Forced fake friendships that often divide
Unbalanced lives
Cliques, Messiness, Pettiness
Dreadful drives
Peer pressure
Fear pressure

Stressed, Burnout, Exhausted

High blood pressure

Long hours
Low pay
Low morale
You can't keep this up everyday
High stressors
High drama
Mucho messiness
The toxicity
The trauma
NO MORE… NOT TODAY
This
    is
      your
Exit Us

Traveling Year Round

Traveling year round
All seasons to and from work
Feeling empty
Blinded by challenges
Traversing in a trance
Surrounded by sounds of turn signals,
humming engines, honking horns…
Sirens singing, chirping birds carelessly
flying trying to cheer you on, wind whistling
Rain rhythmically resounding, sleet tap
dancing on streets, windows, and vehicles
Half dressed trees losing colorful leaves
falling majestically,
while turning flips in the air

Snow falling softly settling on windshields
Staring at us face to face seemingly looking
concerned before blowing or melting away
Bright sun beaming, clouds moving in the
sky
Darkness dominates thoughts and horizons
depending on when we drive
Countenance stuck on stoic
Being driven by daily dread

Traveling year round
All seasons to and from work
Feeling empty
Blinded by challenges
Traversing in a trance

Thoughts While Working

Thoughts of that mortgage
Thoughts of that paycheck that doesn't even
cover your rent
Thoughts of that car note
Thoughts of those monthly bills
Thoughts of massive student loans, medical
bills, and miscellaneous money munchers
Thoughts of that coworker
who refuses to speak
Thoughts of that cliquish colleague
Thoughts of that stupid staff meeting
Thoughts of the second job that awaits you
after your shift is over from job number one
Thoughts of…
The loudest sound you hear regularly are
inner voices pleading
Telling you to quit
and find something else to do
Thoughts of… QUITTING begins to
dominate your mind
until it manifests into your exit

Check Engine Light Bulb Moment

Hands grip the wheel
The "check engine" light has been flashing
more regularly
Hands grip the wheel
You realize the zeal and will to work has
turned to despair
The "check engine" light keeps flashing
You keep ignoring it
Hands grip the wheel
One day, the "check engine" light stays on
Your vehicle begins to shake uncontrollably
Now it can't move at all
Hands let go of the wheel
As you call for a tow, with hazards on
You must face the inevitable after all and
decide to go

A Professional "Show-For"

Who's counting down to the weekend?

Many showed up to work for "show"

A professional "Show-For!"

No paid vacations

No health and dental

No benefits

No doubt,

One foot is already out the door for sure

EXIT US!
A Poetic Look At The Chronicles Of Quitting
© By Anthony J. Butler

Shhhhhh… Many quit quietly before they

make it official

Shhhhhh… Many quit hiring, they just add it

to your schedule

Most days are stressful… stress filled…

chest filled with too much pain

Eyes staring a million miles away…

Trapped

Working in a place with no real end game

Know Hitter

The pandemic hit… You know this
Do you know where you were and what you
were doing?
What in the world is really going on here?
Covid
Fear
Confusion
Frustration
Rage
Agitation
Sadness
Anger
Who's in control?
Censored
Cancelled for critical thinking
Called a conspiracy theorist
What's really going on?
Why are we taking this?
That's it…
We Quit
Your Know Hitter Moment Is Etched In
Your Memory Forever

2020 Vision

March 2020
Our worlds were rocked
Halted exponentially
Plenty of people paused their plans and
stopped
Spring Break was parlayed into schools
closed
Lockdowns
What in the world on lock
Toilet paper and paper towels out of stock
Zooming to meetings
Emotions seeping inward
Downward spirals
Videos going viral
Time Passing…
Tick
Tock
Streaming
Tick
Tock
Online Orders
Tick
Tock

So many people working from home and off
the clock
Many got used to this
Will we go back to work in person?
Many did not

Tick Tock

2020 to present…

Handshakes? People are hesitant

There has been an uptick in elbows touching

and fistbumps

Heads nodding upward greeting people in

unique ways

No contact is how many are addressing each

other and behaving

EXIT US!
A Poetic Look At The Chronicles Of Quitting
© By Anthony J. Butler

You are fully fascinated

You're running on fumes

Mandates

A large percentage of professionals are

lonely with little to no dates man

Shots Fired

Unvaxed

Vaccinated

Quarantines

Masked up

Gloves on

Lives torn

People personifying math problems…

Addition

Subtraction

Multiplication

Division

Wiping down tables and desks

Next day…

Do it again!

Gotta keep everything sanitized and clean

Gotta cough up money to dress down in

t-shirts and jeans

EXIT US!
A Poetic Look At The Chronicles Of Quitting
© By Anthony J. Butler

You are furious and frustrated by the steady

pettines

Work readiness is low

Covid Hits

Schools closed

Schools virtual

Schools hybrid

Some get censored, cancelled, labeled and

social media accounts disabled

We all are tired

No movies or sports

Entertainment looks different

EXIT US!
A Poetic Look At The Chronicles Of Quitting
© By Anthony J. Butler

Small crowds

Big problems

Violence, Crime, Burglaries, Robberies,

Porch Pirates, Murders Rising

Protests

No tests in schools

Multiple Fires… Cities burning… What a
shame… Jobs that used to hire your
neighbors are gone… They fell to the flames

Church services streaming

Driving over faded murals

Heads are rolling and turning

Fast food, wing shortages, weight gains,

Many munching on comfort foods, fries and

Masks… Shots… Boosters…

Suspensions

In a pinch because some have

Pensions pending

Funerals

Elections

Controversies

Politics

Inflation

EXIT US!
A Poetic Look At The Chronicles Of Quitting
© By Anthony J. Butler

A more divided nation

Threats if you don't do this or take that

Oh noooooo!

Are you really saying we have to go?

Manufactured Mayhem

People Are Fully Fascinated

People had enough of this

People just quit and keep some of their

dignity before they are told they must leave

effective immediately

EXIT US!
A Poetic Look At The Chronicles Of Quitting
© By Anthony J. Butler

People personifying math problems…

Addition

Subtraction

Multiplication

Division

We can see clearly now

Insight… Foresight… Hindsight…

2020 Vision

The "DIS" Track

DIS Track lightning hits dominate our playlist and ultimately leads to quits

DIStracted

DISrespected

DISturbed

DISconnected

DIStant

DISciplined

DISappointed

DISengaged

DYSfunction

DIScord between generations

DISregarded

DISdain

DIScounted

DISproportionate

DIScomfort

DIShonest

DISingenuous

DIScredit

DISagreement

DISsatisfied

OVER

UNDER

The OVER UNDER thunder rumbles rock

your core and make you run for the door

Unskilled job openings

Overseas is where some of these jobs be

Overworked

Underpaid

Overwhelmed

Underappreciated and Undervalued

EXIT US!
A Poetic Look At The Chronicles Of Quitting
© By Anthony J. Butler

Overlooked

Understaffed

Overcoming

Undermined

Overjoyed when it's time to leave

EX Factors

The EX factors let you know when it time to

make an EXit Us and go

Excessive

Excuses

Explanations

Expressions

Expose

Examine

Exchange

EXodus

Exit Us

Fed Up

People are sharing epic messages and
vicious videos,

chronicling why they had to go

Working in environments that are just not

Flexible

This lights a fire in other people's souls

People praying and giving themselves pep

talks just to get out of bed most days

They are fed up with doing the job of

multiple people with no increase in pay

EXIT US!
A Poetic Look At The Chronicles Of Quitting
© By Anthony J. Butler

Yelling, hollering, cursing, screaming and

often scheming colleagues and customers

Judgmental, jealous, and just plain insecure

coworkers form a league of their own

These are giant obstacles that can't keep

being tolerated and ignored

You are citing common denominators that
rarely were addressed or accepted for sure

Fed up

You can't take this anymore

You are FED UP

Take The L

Poor Communication

Poor follow up and follow through

is the norm

Paperwork piling

Emails ever present

Phone calls to return

Far too many immaterial meetings

Exhausted… Exhausted… Exhausted…

EXIT US!
A Poetic Look At The Chronicles Of Quitting
© By Anthony J. Butler

Taking too many daily Ls

You finally…

Lost your zeal to work in this place

You Lost it

You Left Because You Just Lost it

You just Took The L

The Weather

Winds are changing

Opportunities are blowing your direction

Dark clouds are moving out

Sunny days are ahead

The long range forecast is full of favorable

work conditions just for you

Pray and move as God instructs you

Winds are changing

Opportunities are blowing your direction

Bottom Line

From the top down,

We constantly hear about how the bottom
line drives decisions

The bottom line when met screams success
and precision

The bottom line is fueled by…

Seeing you more as some sort of a number
thing rather than

ONE WHOLE human being

You are far more than just numbers and
digits

Cutie pie charts

Great looking graphs

Pretty percentages

Dissecting decimals

Forecasting fractions

The residual from the beautiful visuals

Bottomline

Data, stats, and financial gains are

emphasized over employees' mental health

EXIT US!
A Poetic Look At The Chronicles Of Quitting
© By Anthony J. Butler

Data, stats, and financial gain are

emphasized over employees' bank accounts

and wealth

Employees are trying but they are dying

each day a slow, painful, pain filled death…

That's why employers can't really recruit

That's why employers can't retain and

sustain those who want to joyfully remain

The one sided laser focus is fastly funneling

many feet out the door

EXIT US!
A Poetic Look At The Chronicles Of Quitting
© By Anthony J. Butler

The top gets the primary portion of profits

The bottom maybe gets you a living wage

The rich get richer and this sets the stage

For…

An out of balance and out of human touch

research based workplace

Has led to many people to say,

"We search'" for a new place to work where

we are valued

Bottomline

A Bevy of Bullies

The belts get brought out in many staff meetings

A bevy of bully power tripping bosses have you sitting on egg shells

A bevy of bully power tripping bosses have you biting fingernails

A bevy of bully power tripping bosses have you sitting through threat filled meetings

EXIT US!
A Poetic Look At The Chronicles Of Quitting
© By Anthony J. Butler

Too many threats

You need to do this

Don't do that

You can be replaced at the drop of a hat

When you permit this

You promote this bullying foolishness

The atmosphere accelerates and fuels this

which leads to more and more quits

It's Your Fault

You try to adjust and manufacture that
growth mindset

But your mind keeps drifting a million miles
away seething

Doubting yourself and sometimes you cave
in and start believing…

It's your fault

It's your fault people label you insensitive
and cold

This is a trip

It's your fault

when relationships are not built

EXIT US!
A Poetic Look At The Chronicles Of Quitting
© By Anthony J. Butler

You are bending over backwards

doing cartwheels to connect

You and many other workers sometimes

succumb to drinking, vaping, smoking,

Playing video games, streaming shows,

binges and popping pills

Truth be told,

when you dare to ask for some support…

You often get interrogated and insulted

Of course it's your fault

Penalties

Far too many professionals get reprimanded

and called out for penalties,

For not buying into "we are a family"

Many get penalized for trying to leave

They have to pay fees, lose certifications,

this leads to the trauma rising

The drama is rising more

Make this make sense

and connect these dots

What is this all about?

They want to scream and shout

EXIT US!
A Poetic Look At The Chronicles Of Quitting
© By Anthony J. Butler

They are penalized, censored and cancelled

for speaking facts

If more people told the whole truth and

nothing but the truth

A large percentage of their bosses will tell

them what to think, not how to think

They push them out the door and assign

security to watch them as they pack

Helicopters

Smothering

Hovering

Obsolete observations and

Evil evaluations gone wild

You are getting low marks

Wow

Meanwhile

Like clockwork…

Here we go

You are told to work overtime again

Now… Who's gonna watch your child?

You are broke in more ways than one

This is no fun day after day

It's time to walk away from the…

Smothering

Hovering

What? The Helicopters Strike Again

Can't Wait To Get Home

You arrive to work and immediately

can't wait to get home

You don't get many breaks

Your hair is falling out and you are routinely

looking disheveled

You are wearing crumpled up clothes loaded

with wrinkles

You are rocking crooked glasses

EXIT US!
A Poetic Look At The Chronicles Of Quitting
© By Anthony J. Butler

You can't see your way out

You and others can't wait to get home

You want to quit

You've put it off for a long time

But today might be it

Gaslighting

People are playing mind games

Messing with minds

Gaslighting goes on often

You ain't crazy and making this up

No doubt

Some people make you think that something

was slipped in your cup is half empty

This is not complicated

EXIT US!
A Poetic Look At The Chronicles Of Quitting
© By Anthony J. Butler

Look

Simply put

You get lit up so many times that part

of your work uniform requires a gasmask

Putting on this gas mask daily

is not sustainable

This is why you and many others don't last

Artificial Appreciation

You don't want another one of these shallow

appreciation months

It's like Artificial Intelligence is activated

and present

Human touch, authenticity and genuineness

is waning

Manufactured moments of mundane moving

messages don't move your feet

No more token gifts or presents

No more cute slogan filled treats

No more artificial appreciation

and over explaining

No more coffee mugs

No more gum

No more gummy bears, potato chips, snacks,

and tote bags

No more candies, with little notes saying…

"Stick To This" "You're So Sweet"

Just STOP it

No more catchy phrases and clichés

This is an absolute joke

Artificial appreciation

is Not Appreciated by you

The Support Card

I must say this

I must speak

Stop guilting them to give up their days off

in the name of teamwork

If you wanna really help

Support them

You can start by treating people like a whole

professional

Pay them some real respect

Support them

Give them some consistent support

EXIT US!
A Poetic Look At The Chronicles Of Quitting
© By Anthony J. Butler

Get them a meaningful pay increase loaded

with benefits, empathy and flexibility

The grades are in

It's support card time

Support them

Really try to put on their shoes

Walk out the journey of their feet in these

worklife streets

EXIT US!
A Poetic Look At The Chronicles Of Quitting
© By Anthony J. Butler

See where their feet take them each day

Each week, each commute, each night

They rarely get a good night's rest

Another loss

Defeat

Sleep is disturbed

They're tired

Give them some consistent support

Support them

The grades are in

It's support card time

Really Support Them

Toxic Positivinese

If you were to get twenty dollars for every

time you hear "Toxic Positivinese"

You would be rich

Robotic rhetoric

It's all bite with no teeth

"Toxic Positivinese"

"Normalcy"

"Let's Stay Vigilant"

"We Are In This together"

"We Are Going To Get Through This"

"We're a family"
"I'm Super Excited, Super Pumped,
 Super Ready, Super___________"
"Let's Go Team"
"Laser Focus"
"Open Door Policy"
"You Are Welcome, Belong…"
"Reach Out For Help"
"Awesome"

When staff hears clichés all day, it pushes
them away

Especially when these clichés are smothered
in hypocrisy

Not Safe

Your safety is compromised

You are reluctant and/or refuse to work the

night shift because you might get hit

Doing this job might cost you your life

You just want to make it home alive

Put in dangerous positions day after day

Abusive customers, clients, colleagues

and management

Bullets bouncing off cars and buildings

Bullets bouncing off people in public places,

in stores, in schools

Bullets bouncing off people at games and

track meets

Enduring verbal, emotional, psychological

and sometimes physical abuse

People constantly cursing you out

Who has been robbed, chased, threatened,

held at gunpoint and more while working?

Who carries a gun, firearm, taser, pepper

spray, another type of weapon and/or mace?

Of course the sirens are hoarse from singing

all day and night around your workplace

This job is unsafe

Toll Bridges

Your family takes the toll

You are constantly pulled away

Should you walk away?

The toll pushes you to look for a way out

Your health takes the toll

Your peace takes the toll

You pray for direction

You talk and listen

You vent and ask God questions

Should you stay or leave?

EXIT US!
A Poetic Look At The Chronicles Of Quitting
© By Anthony J. Butler

Tired of being tired and worn out

Your life is more important than the toll

bridges no doubt

You decide to skip these toll bridges and

find a new career route

Un Un

Unnoticed

Underestimated

Not acknowledged for your steady mastery

Unreasonable and unrealistic expectations
are the norm

Working in unsafe environments and unsafe
conditions

Ongoing ugly and unhealthy conversations

Unbearable pressure

Unreal workload

Understandably… You are uncomfortable
working here for much longer

Un Un…

It's time to quit and run

"10-4"

Take this test

Ask 10 people to describe their profession in
4 words

Most will share words like,

Stressful

Overwhelming

Exhausting

Burnout

We wonder why so many leave

Take this test

Go to 10 people

Ask them to describe their profession in 4
words please

Do They Even Know?

Do they even know who they're talking to?

Do they even know your name?

Do they even know what you really do?

Maybe if your boss really knew who you were

Maybe if your boss really knew what you did and what you went through

Maybe if we had one on one meetings throughout the year

They would have treated you differently with more dignity

You probably would have stayed longer too and you might still be working here

Complicated

This is complicated

Lines blurred

Boundaries crossed

You shouldn't have dated another coworker,

trainee or your boss

Now you are dealing with the fallout

You actually enjoyed everything about this

job, the hours and the pay

However, because of the complications

It's best that you get lost before it's too late

This is complicated

Politics

Are you on the other side?

No matter what color you roll with and ride

Are you woke, sleep, taking naps, dozing

and everything in between?

What you can deduce and ascertain is…

If your political party, views and values are

opposite of the majority at work

This most likely will be the very thing that

makes you a target

Constantly catching all the heat

and all the smoke

This causes many to quit

Office… Party…

Politics

Little To No Training

First day

You are just happy to be here

You are thrown head first into a fast paced

atmosphere

With little to no training

Sometimes the training is full speed,

but lacks quality

You are expected to take the reins and

function at a high level

You are constantly yelled at

You tolerate temper tantrums throughout the

week… You just can't get used to this

So you quit

In Plain Sight

Some leaders do not attempt to hide who
their "ride or dies" are
They go out of their way to announce with
words and actions that these people are…
Their friends
Their shining stars
Their ears
Their eyes
Their mouth pieces
This signals to others that these work friends
will get preferential treatment
Some will do double duties as spies
That's why so many will
eventually leave quick

Not Buying

The staff doesn't buy in
The culture and climate is terrible
The leader is not respected
Work conditions are unbearable
The staff knows it.
Chaos creeps and sets in
Many "mini" leaders are running around,
speaking for the leader
Making decisions like the leader
This leads to BIG confusion and a lack of
buy in

Present Yet Absent

In addition to all the quits…

Don't forget those who are present the vast

majority of days physically,

Yet absent the vast majority of days

mentally, emotionally and creatively

People are present, yet absent, doing the

bare minimum to survive

Bouncing around from job to job and career
to career for weeks, months or years

My… My… My…

Playing musical chairs
until they are out of here

Cruise Control

You hate working here or anywhere because
you can't cruise and coast

You have the audacity to complain when the
work gets heavy
Because you are comfortable doing the least
yet getting paid the most

You hate working here or anywhere because
you can't manipulate and control

So

You quit and will keep quitting if people
don't allow you to keep it on
cruise
    control

Fake Statements

Let me say this about all of the statements

Don't make this if you're gonna fake this

Some are making statements out of peer

pressure and fear pressure

Afraid others will look and listen

and begin to see their true colors

and hear better

The latest senseless atrocity

Has so many coming out of the woods with

apologies

Time will reveal

if this is heartfelt or hypocrisy

EXIT US!
A Poetic Look At The Chronicles Of Quitting
© By Anthony J. Butler

Will the work statements be the start of a

root level movement

or just another mockery?

Sometimes excellent people leave because

the fake statements are a botchery

It Shouldn't Take

It shouldn't take a pandemic for people to recognize…

Your game

Your craft

Your championship banners hanging from the rafters year after year

It shouldn't take you being absent for others to appreciate your presence

It shouldn't take you quitting before people value your impactful work and position

Users

They got what they wanted from you then
labeled you a loser

Has anyone ever used you to elevate their
career?

After you helped them
You served your purpose
Then you are out of here

The number 2 is secretly plotting behind the
number 1's back

Smiling in their face :)

While simultaneously using them until just
at the right moment and then…
Here comes an ambush…
An unexpected slap in the face
An epic sneak attack
Has anyone ever used you to elevate their
career?

Clues and Breadcrumbs

You've been dropping hints for a minute

Showing up and putting in the work
but your heart's not in it

Forever foreshadowing your silhouette
leaving this place

You and your shadow will eventually go

No need to hire a private investigator or a
detective to look for you when you
disappear

You've been dropping clues, hints and
leaving breadcrumbs for months and years

Letting people know that sooner or later…

You are outta here

Exit Survey

You finally get to say how YOU REALLY

FEEL on this exit survey

So, they really want to know why you quit?

Ok… This is it

You ran like an olympic sprinter

You broke world records to get out of here

Working anywhere else

would be a breath of fresh air

Your workplace is full of people who refuse

to listen

EXIT US!
A Poetic Look At The Chronicles Of Quitting
© By Anthony J. Butler

Common sense is missing

Leaders constantly gone fishing

Knife wounds are evident in multiple backs

and there is a whole lot of kissing up

Working with snakes

not great communication,

but there is a whole lot of hissing stuff

You just can't fit in…

EXIT US!
A Poetic Look At The Chronicles Of Quitting
© By Anthony J. Butler

High work volume

Low pay

Things were not okay most days

Unprofessional

Unstable Leadership,

Toxic Workplace,

High Turnover Rate,

Excuses…

What more can you say?

Will root level changes be made after

someone reads your Exit Survey?

It's Up To You

It's very difficult to
Recruit

Retain

And

Joyfully Remain
in work environments that keep doing the
same troublesome things
that push people out the door

After you examine the common
denominators and root reasons why so many
people quit…

It's up to you what you'll do with this

www.ingramcontent.com/pod-product-compliance
Lightning Source LLC
Chambersburg PA
CBHW071607270726
48661CB00019B/1642